FLUENCY MINI-LESSONS

FLUENCY

Grade 1

Newmark™
LEARNING

Newmark Learning • 629 Fifth Avenue • Pelham, NY • 10803

Newmark Learning

629 Fifth Avenue • Pelham, NY • 10803

ISBN: 978-1-60719-062-2

For ordering information, call Toll-Free 1-877-279-8388 or visit our Web site at www.newmarklearning.com.

Table of Contents

Instructions. 4

Mini-Lessons

1. Speed/Pacing: Fast 6
2. Speed/Pacing: Slow 8
3. Speed/Pacing: Varied 10
4. Pausing: Short Pause 12
5. Pausing: Full Stop 14
6. Pausing: Text Structure
   and Organization 16
7. Inflection/Intonation: Pitch 18
8. Inflection/Intonation: Volume 20
9. Inflection/Intonation: Stress 22
10. Phrasing: High-Frequency
    Word Phrases. 24
11. Phrasing: Subject/
    Predicate Phrases 26
12. Phrasing: Prepositional Phrases 28
13. Expression: Anticipation and Mood . . 30
14. Expression: Characterization
    and Feelings. 32
15. Expression: Dramatic Expression 34

Mini-Lesson Transparency Blackline Masters

1. Speed/Pacing: Fast 36
2. Speed/Pacing: Slow 37
3. Speed/Pacing: Varied 38
4. Pausing: Short Pause 39
5. Pausing: Full Stop 40
6. Pausing: Text Structure
   and Organization 41
7. Inflection/Intonation: Pitch 42
8. Inflection/Intonation: Volume 43
9. Inflection/Intonation: Stress 44
10. Phrasing: High-Frequency
    Word Phrases. 45
11. Phrasing: Subject/
    Predicate Phrases 46
12. Phrasing: Prepositional Phrases 47
13. Expression: Anticipation and Mood . . 48
14. Expression: Characterization
    and Feelings. 49
15. Expression: Dramatic Expression. . . . 50

Fluency Rubric. 51

Fluency Self-Assessment
Master Checklist 52

Welcome to Newmark Learning's Fluency Mini-Lessons Series. Each grade-level book in this series provides fifteen unique and explicit mini-lessons for teaching the many facets of fluency. The model-guide-apply approach of each mini-lesson gives teachers the tools to help students focus on the fluency skills they need to improve comprehension.

Fluency Research

Fluency is the ability to read a text accurately and quickly. Fluent readers recognize words automatically. They group words into phrases to help them gain the meaning of what they read. Fluent readers also read aloud using prosody—the technical term for reading with expressiveness—with little or no effort.

Fluency is a vital skill because it directly relates to comprehension. Research from the National Reading Panel concludes that explicit fluency instruction is an essential component of reading instruction. The mini-lessons in the Fluency Mini-Lessons Series reflect the most current research on how to effectively teach reading fluency skills.

The Facets of Reading Fluency

Although much instructional emphasis is placed on reading accurately and at a grade-appropriate rate, a truly fluent reader has mastered all of the key elements of fluency: speed and pacing, pausing, phrasing, inflection and intonation, and reading with expression. Each of these elements is addressed within this book.

Speed and pacing is reading faster or slower to help show the meaning of the passage.

Pausing is using the words and punctuation to figure out when to take a short or long break while reading.

Inflection and intonation is changing your voice—high or low, loud or soft—to help show the meaning of the passage, as well as knowing when to emphasize certain words.

Phrasing is reading related groups of words together to help the passage make sense.

Expression is using different voices, facial expressions, and body language to help show the meaning of the passage.

Two other important skills included in the mini-lessons are **accuracy**—reading the words correctly—and **integration**—combining all the skills in a way that shows the reader understands the text.

As students read aloud, use the Fluency Rubric (page 51) to help choose the areas in which students need additional study and practice. You may also use the rubric as a teaching tool by modeling each description so students know what to expect.

Each mini-lesson includes an accompanying reading passage to help teach the skill.

Following are the steps for presenting a fluency mini-lesson:

Before

1. Study the lesson objectives.

2. Make an overhead transparency and student copies of the mini-lesson passage.

3. Make student copies of the Fluency Self-Assessment Master Checklist (page 52).

4. Create a wall chart or individual bookmarks with the questions on the mini-lesson's Self-Assessment Checklist.

During

1. Describe the skill. Model the skill using the passage on the overhead transparency. Help students create a chart that lists the most important ideas about the skill.

2. Distribute the student copies of the passage and Fluency Self-Assessment Master Checklist. Assist students as they practice reading the passage as a group and answer questions about their reading.

3. Allow time for individuals or partners to practice the skill by reading level-appropriate texts or passages from Newmark Learning's Independent Fluency Practice Passages series, which includes precisely leveled fiction, nonfiction, monologue, and dialogue passages. Use the mini-lesson prompt list to assist and encourage students as they practice.

4. Invite individuals or partners to perform a sentence or two from their reading, paying special attention to the mini-lesson skill.

After

1. Continue monitoring students' progress using the Fluency Rubric (page 51).
2. Continue providing mini-lessons based on students' learning needs.

Speed/Pacing: Fast

Objectives

Students will:

- read a rhythmic text at a fast pace

- utilize punctuation cues

- demonstrate understanding of the text through purposeful pacing

- use effective pacing to make their reading sound like talking

---

Mini-Lesson BLM 1, page 36

Miss Mary Mack

Miss Mary Mack, Mack, Mack
All dressed in black, black, black
With silver buttons, buttons, buttons
All down her back, back, back.

She asked her mother, mother, mother
For fifty cents, cents, cents
To see the elephant, elephant, elephant
Jump the fence, fence, fence.

He jumped so high, high, high
He touched the sky, sky, sky
And didn't come back, back, back
Till the fourth of July, July, July.

Anchor Chart

Speed/Pacing

- We read different kinds of texts at different speeds.

- We read easy parts faster and hard parts slower.

- We match our pacing to what the author is saying.

- Reading too fast makes the reading hard to understand.

- Reading too slowly does not sound natural.

- No matter what speed we use to read, we pay attention to punctuation.

Introduce the Skill (10 minutes)

- **Say:** *We read different kinds of texts at different speeds. Pacing is the speed we use to read. We read things like tongue twisters and rhymes quickly to keep the rhythm going. We read things like directions slowly to make sure we don't miss any steps. Sometimes we read different parts of a text at different speeds, too. We read the easy parts faster, and we read the hard parts slower. We also think about what the author is saying. How would you read a sentence about an exciting race? (quickly) How would you read a sentence about something sad? (slowly) Good readers pace their speed to match what they are reading. Pacing shows that we understand what we are reading. Pacing helps our listeners understand what we are reading, too.*

- Display a transparency of the fluency mini-lesson passage BLM on the overhead and read the title. **Say:** *This is a hand-clap rhyme. I want to keep the rhythm going, so I need to read it quickly. I can read faster if I don't point to the words with my finger. I don't want to read too fast, though. I want everyone to understand what I am reading, so I mustn't run the words together. I must take time to pause at the commas and periods, too.*

- Have students listen and follow along as you read the rhyme aloud quickly and rhythmically, pausing briefly at each comma and period. Then **say:** *I will read the first verse of the rhyme again. This time, I will read it very slowly. Listen closely. Read the first verse in a slow, word-by-word manner.*

- **Ask:** Which speed did you like best? Why?

- Invite students to help you create a class Anchor Chart to remind them how good readers use speed and pacing. (See the example provided.) When you are finished, ask students to echo-read the entire chart. Then post the chart in the classroom for future reference.

Group Guided Practice (15 minutes)

- Distribute the BLM for Miss Mary Mack. Divide students into two groups and ask them to choral-read the rhyme with you one or more times, alternating lines by group. Next, allow the groups to choral-read their parts without your assistance.

- Distribute the Fluency Self-Assessment Master Checklist BLM from page 52. Then review the assessment criteria for speed/pacing and integration (see the checklist, right). Ask students to give a thumbs-up or thumbs-down on each question based on the group's choral-reading. Discuss their responses.

- Pair students and ask them to read Miss Mary Mack together one or more times, alternating lines. If time allows, invite them to try the rhyme as a hand-clap activity.

- Ask students to rate themselves on specific fluency skills covered in this lesson using their master checklists.

- Check comprehension by asking student partners to discuss the following: Which parts of the rhyme could be real? Why? Which parts of the rhyme are make-believe? How do you know?

Individual/Partner Practice (15 minutes)

- Ask students to practice their oral reading skills by reading texts at their independent reading levels. You may want to use the leveled passages in Newmark Learning's Independent Fluency Practice Series.

- Carefully monitor students' progress, using the appropriate prompts (provided in the sidebar, right) to support their oral reading.

- Remind students to use the Self-Assessment Checklist to rate their oral reading skills and note any areas they might need to work on.

Performance (5 minutes)

- Invite individuals or partners to read a sentence or two from their fluency practice tests aloud for the class, paying special attention to speed and pacing.

Self-Assessment Checklist

Speed/Pacing
- [ ] Did my speed and pacing match the kind of text I was reading?
- [ ] Did my speed and pacing match what the author was saying?
- [ ] Did I read with a natural talking voice?
- [ ] Did I slow my reading down when appropriate?
- [ ] Did I pay attention to punctuation?

Integration
- [ ] Did I read the words right?
- [ ] Did I read with expression?
- [ ] Did my reading sound like talking?
- [ ] Did I understand what I read?

Speed/Pacing Prompts

Goal Oriented
- Listen to me read. Can you read it like I do?
- Listen to how I read this. I am going to read this faster.
- Listen to how I read this. I am going to read this slower.
- Listen to my voice as I read the next sentence. Am I reading at a fluent pace?

Directive and Corrective Feedback
- Read these words faster.
- Read these words slower.
- Try that again and read slower.
- Try that again and read faster.
- Try moving your eyes quicker so you can read more words together.
- Read the text again and make it sound like you are talking.

Self-Monitoring and Reflection
- How did you pace your reading?
- Did you read that too fast or too slow?
- What did you do to read that faster/slower?
- How did you vary your pace in that passage?
- What did you notice about your reading?
- What made you read slower or faster?
- Where did you read too fast/slow?
- Where did you read at the right pace?

Validating and Confirming
- I liked the way you read it faster that time.
- I liked the way you slowed your reading down that time.
- Good job at varying your pace in the passage.
- You read at an appropriate rate. Great job!

Speed/Pacing: Slow

Objectives

Students will:
- read a set of directions at a slow pace
- utilize punctuation cues
- demonstrate understanding of the text through purposeful pacing
- use effective pacing to make their reading sound like talking

Mini-Lesson BLM 2, page 37

Paper Cup Telephone

1. Get two paper cups. Get a pushpin. Get some string.
2. Poke a hole in the bottom of each paper cup.
3. Wiggle the pushpin to make the holes a little bigger.
4. Put the string through the holes.
5. Tie knots in the ends of the string.
6. Hand one cup to a partner. Tell your partner to put the cup to their ear.
7. Stretch out the string. Talk into your cup.
8. Now let your partner talk to you. You've made a paper cup telephone!

Anchor Chart

Speed/Pacing
- We read different kinds of texts at different speeds.
- We read easy parts faster and hard parts slower.
- We match our pacing to what the author is saying.
- Reading too fast makes the reading hard to understand.
- Reading too slowly does not sound natural.
- No matter what speed we use to read, we pay attention to punctuation.

Introduce the Skill (10 minutes)

- **Say:** *We have learned that we read different kinds of texts at different speeds. This is called pacing. Sometimes we read different parts of a text at different speeds, too. We read faster or slower depending on how easy or hard the text is and to match what the author is saying. Good readers use pacing to help their reading sound right and make sense to themselves and others.*

- Display a transparency of the fluency mini-lesson passage BLM on the overhead and read the title. **Say:** *This is a set of directions. We read directions slowly to make sure we don't miss any steps. We also pause when we see punctuation. I don't want to read too slowly, though. Reading too slowly does not sound natural.*

- Gather two paper cups, a pushpin, and some string. Have students listen and follow along as you read the directions aloud slowly, stopping to demonstrate each step. Display your finished project and **ask:** *What if I read all the directions very quickly before I started making the paper cup telephone? Do you think the telephone would turn out the same?* Allow student discussion, and then point out that you might not have understood what to do or you might have forgotten a step by the time you got to the end of the directions.

- Reread the class Anchor Chart together to remind students how good readers use speed and pacing. (See the example provided.)

Group Guided Practice (15 minutes)

- Distribute the BLM for *Paper Cup Telephone*. Ask students to echo-read each line, and then have them choral-read the directions with you. Next, allow the group to choral-read the directions without your assistance.

- Distribute the Fluency Self-Assessment Master Checklist from page 52. Then review the assessment criteria for speed/pacing and integration (see the checklist, right). Ask students to give a thumbs-up or thumbs-down on each question based on the group's choral-reading. Discuss their responses.

- Pair students and ask them to read *Paper Cup Telephone* together, alternating lines. If time allows, invite them to carry out the directions as well.

- Ask students to rate themselves on specific fluency skills covered in this lesson using their master checklists.

- Check comprehension by asking student partners to discuss the following: *How do you make a paper cup telephone? Why do you wiggle the pushpin? Why do you tie knots at the ends of the string?*

Individual/Partner Practice (15 minutes)

- Ask students to practice their oral reading skills by reading texts at their independent reading levels. You may want to use the leveled passages in Newmark Learning's Independent Fluency Practice Series.

- Carefully monitor students' progress, using the appropriate prompts (provided in the sidebar, right) to support their oral reading.

Remind students to use the Self-Assessment Checklist to rate their oral reading skills and note any areas they might need to work on.

Performance (5 minutes)

- Invite individuals or partners to read a sentence or two from their fluency practice texts aloud for the class, paying special attention to speed and pacing.

Self-Assessment Checklist

Speed/Pacing

☐ Did my speed and pacing match the kind of text I was reading?
☐ Did my speed and pacing match what the author was saying?
☐ Did I read with a natural talking voice?
☐ Did I slow my reading down when appropriate?
☐ Did I pay attention to punctuation?

Integration

☐ Did I read the words right?
☐ Did I read with expression?
☐ Did my reading sound like talking?
☐ Did I understand what I read?

Speed/Pacing Prompts

Goal Oriented
- Listen to me read. Can you read it like I do?
- Listen to how I read this. I am going to read this faster.
- Listen to how I read this. I am going to read this slower.
- Listen to my voice as I read the next sentence. Am I reading at a fluent pace?

Directive and Corrective Feedback
- Read these words faster.
- Read these words slower.
- Try that again and read slower.
- Try that again and read faster.
- Try moving your eyes quicker so you can read more words together.
- Read the text again and make it sound like you are talking.

Self-Monitoring and Reflection
- How did you pace your reading?
- Did you read that too fast or too slow?
- What did you do to read that faster/slower?
- How did you vary your pace in that passage?
- What did you notice about your reading?
- What made you read slower or faster?
- Where did you read too fast/slow?
- Where did you read at the right pace?

Validating and Confirming
- I liked the way you read it faster that time.
- I liked the way you slowed your reading down that time.
- Good job at varying your pace in the passage.
- You read at an appropriate rate. Great job!

Speed/Pacing: Varied

Objectives

Students will:
- read a dialogue at a varied pace

- utilize punctuation cues

- demonstrate understanding of the text through purposeful pacing

- use effective pacing to make their reading sound like talking

Mini-Lesson BLM 3, page 38

Things I Like To Do
Speaker 1: I like to go for long walks with my dog.
Speaker 2: I like to run in the yard with my dog.
Speaker 1: I like to play board games that take all afternoon.
Speaker 2: I like to play computer games with lots of action. Wham! Zam!
Speaker 1: I like to bake cookies with my granddad.
Speaker 2: I like to grab a quick burger with my big brother.
Speaker 1: I like to learn new words. Today I learned to say au-to-bi-o-gra-phy.
Speaker 2: I like words, too. Did you know that some people say soda and some people say pop?
Speaker 1 and **Speaker 2:** Y...a...w...n. I like to take a nap. See you later!

Anchor Chart

Speed/Pacing
- We read different kinds of texts at different speeds.

- We read easy parts faster and hard parts slower.

- We match our pacing to what the author is saying.

- Reading too fast makes the reading hard to understand.

- Reading too slowly does not sound natural.

- No matter what speed we use to read, we pay attention to punctuation.

Introduce the Skill (10 minutes)

- **Say**: *We have learned that we read different kinds of texts at different speeds. This is called pacing. Sometimes we read different parts of a text at different speeds, too. We read faster or slower depending on how easy or hard the text is and to match what the author is saying. Good readers use pacing to help their reading sound right and make sense to themselves and others.*

- Display a transparency of the fluency mini-lesson passage BLM on the overhead and read the title. **Say:** *This is a dialogue. The first speaker likes to do slow, relaxing activities, so I'll read those parts slower. The second speaker likes fast, lively activities, so I'll read those parts faster. I'll also look for easy and hard words and pay close attention to the punctuation to know when to speed up or slow down.*

- Have students listen and follow along as you read the passage aloud, varying your speed to match what the speakers are saying and utilizing punctuation cues. Then **say**: *I will read part of the dialogue again. This time, I will read every word at the same speed.* Read the first few parts in a slow, word-by-word manner.

- **Ask:** *Which way makes the dialogue sound better? Why?*

- Reread the class Anchor Chart together to remind students how good readers use speed and pacing. (See the example provided.)

Group Guided Practice (15 minutes)

- Distribute the BLM for *Things I Like To Do*. Divide students into Speaker 1 and Speaker 2 groups and ask them to choral-read their parts with you one or more times. Next, allow the groups to choral-read their parts without your assistance.

- Distribute the Fluency Self-Assessment Master Checklist BLM from page 52. Then review the assessment criteria for speed/pacing and integration (see the checklist, right). Ask students to give a thumbs-up or thumbs-down on each question based on the group's choral-reading. Discuss their responses.

- Pair students, and then put two pairs together. Assign one pair as Speaker 1 and one pair as Speaker 2, and invite them to read *Things I Like To Do* together one or more times.

- Ask students to rate themselves on specific fluency skills covered in this lesson using their master checklists.

- Check comprehension by asking student partners to discuss the following: *Think about the things Speaker 1 and Speaker 2 like to do. Which activity do you like best? Why?*

Individual/Partner Practice (15 minutes)

- Ask students to practice their oral reading skills by reading texts at their independent reading levels. You may want to use the leveled passages in Newmark Learning's Independent Fluency Practice Series.

- Carefully monitor students' progress, using the appropriate prompts (provided in the sidebar, right) to support their oral reading.

- Remind students to use the Self-Assessment Checklist to rate their oral reading skills and note any areas they might need to work on.

Performance (5 minutes)

- Invite individuals or partners to read a sentence or two from their fluency practice texts aloud for the class, paying special attention to speed and pacing.

Self-Assessment Checklist

Speed/Pacing
- [ ] Did my speed and pacing match the kind of text I was reading?
- [ ] Did my speed and pacing match what the author was saying?
- [ ] Did I read with a natural talking voice?
- [ ] Did I slow my reading down when appropriate?
- [ ] Did I pay attention to punctuation?

Integration
- [ ] Did I read the words right?
- [ ] Did I read with expression?
- [ ] Did my reading sound like talking?
- [ ] Did I understand what I read?

Speed/Pacing Prompts

Goal Oriented
- Listen to me read. Can you read it like I do?
- Listen to how I read this. I am going to read this faster.
- Listen to how I read this. I am going to read this slower.
- Listen to my voice as I read the next sentence. Am I reading at a fluent pace?

Directive and Corrective Feedback
- Read these words faster.
- Read these words slower.
- Try that again and read slower.
- Try that again and read faster.
- Try moving your eyes quicker so you can read more words together.
- Read the text again and make it sound like you are talking.

Self-Monitoring and Reflection
- How did you pace your reading?
- Did you read that too fast or too slow?
- What did you do to read that faster/slower?
- How did you vary your pace in that passage?
- What did you notice about your reading?
- What made you read slower or faster?
- Where did you read too fast/slow?
- Where did you read at the right pace?

Validating and Confirming
- I liked the way you read it faster that time.
- I liked the way you slowed your reading down that time.
- Good job at varying your pace in the passage.
- You read at an appropriate rate. Great job!

Pausing: Short Pause

Objectives

Students will:
- utilize punctuation to signal short pauses while reading
- demonstrate understanding of the text through purposeful pausing
- use effective pausing to make their reading sound like talking

Mini-Lesson BLM 4, page 39

Snow

Many people like snow.

Kids like to go sledding, build a snowman, and throw snowballs.

People take lots of pictures because the trees look so pretty.

People can ski on the fresh snow, called powder.

Snowplow drivers have to work hard, but they feel good helping people.

Some people don't like snow, though.

Snow makes things harder for mail carriers, farmers, builders, and pilots.

Do you like snow?

Anchor Chart

Pausing
- We do not run all our words together.
- We pause, or rest, between some words.
- Pausing divides sentences into meaningful parts.
- Pausing makes our reading easier to understand.
- Punctuation helps us figure out when to pause.
- Punctuation helps us figure out how long to pause.

Introduce the Skill (10 minutes)

- **Say:** *When we talk, we do not run all our words together. Instead, we pause, or rest, between some words. The pause may be very short, or the pause may be longer. Pausing helps us divide our sentences into meaningful parts. Pausing helps our listeners understand what we are saying, too. In reading, the punctuation helps us figure out when to pause. One kind of punctuation that signals a short pause is a comma. We take a little break at a comma before reading on.*

- Display a transparency of the fluency mini-lesson passage BLM on the overhead and read the title. **Say:** *This passage is about snow. The author uses commas to show us when to pause. A short pause at each comma helps the sentences sound right and make sense.*

- Have students listen and follow along as you read the passage aloud, pausing briefly at each comma. Then **say:** *I will read the second sentence three times. First, I will read it the way I did before, pausing at the commas. Next, I will read it without pausing. Finally, I will ignore the commas and pause in different places.* Read the second sentence as written, in a word-by-word manner, and with awkward pauses. (Kids like to / go sledding build / a snowman and / throw snowballs)

- **Ask:** *Which way is easiest to understand? Why?*

- Invite students to help you create a class Anchor Chart to remind them how good readers use pausing. (See the example provided.) When you are finished, ask students to echo-read the entire chart. Then post the chart in the classroom for future reference.

Group Guided Practice (15 minutes)

- Distribute the BLM for *Snow*. Ask students to echo-read each sentence, and then have them choral-read the passage with you. Next, allow the group to choral-read the passage without your assistance.

- Distribute the Fluency Self-Assessment Master Checklist BLM from page 52. Then review the assessment criteria for pausing and integration (see the checklist, right). Ask students to give a thumbs-up or thumbs-down on each question based on the group's choral-reading. Discuss their responses.

- Pair students and ask them to read *Snow* together one or more times, alternating lines.

- Ask students to rate themselves on specific fluency skills covered in this lesson using their master checklists.

- Check comprehension by asking student partners to discuss the following: *Who are some people who like snow? Why? Who are some people who don't like snow? Why? How would you answer the question at the end of the passage? Why?*

Individual/Partner Practice (15 minutes)

- Ask students to practice their oral reading skills by reading texts at their independent reading levels. You may want to use the leveled passages in Newmark Learning's Independent Fluency Practice Series.

- Carefully monitor students' progress, using the appropriate prompts (provided in the sidebar, right) to support their oral reading.

- Remind students to use the Self-Assessment Checklist to rate their oral reading skills and note any areas they might need to work on.

Performance (5 minutes)

- Invite individuals or partners to read a sentence or two from their fluency practice texts aloud for the class, paying special attention to pausing.

Self-Assessment Checklist

Pausing

☐ Did I pause to keep from running all my words together?

☐ Did I pause in the correct locations?

☐ Did I pause for the appropriate length of time?

☐ Did I pause to help my reading make sense?

☐ Did I use punctuation to help me figure out when to pause?

Integration

☐ Did I read the words right?

☐ Did I read the words at the right speed?

☐ Did I read with expression?

☐ Did my reading sound like talking?

☐ Did I understand what I read?

Pausing Prompts

Goal Oriented

- Listen to me read this. Can you hear me take a little breath at the comma (semicolon, dash, colon, ellipsis)?
- The period (question mark, exclamation point) means your voice makes a full stop.
- When I make a short pause, I don't stop completely and break the flow of my reading.
- When I finish a sentence, I make a full stop before continuing my reading.
- Notice what I do when I see a(n) comma (semicolon, dash, colon, ellipsis). My reading pauses briefly, and then continues to help to make ideas clear as I read.
- Notice what I do when I see a(n) period (question mark, exclamation point). My reading pauses with a full stop to show that I've read a complete sentence or idea.

Directive and Corrective Feedback

- Make a full stop at the period (question mark, exclamation point).
- Take a little breath when you see a(n) comma (semicolon, dash, colon, ellipsis).
- Read it like this with a full stop after the word.

Self-Monitoring and Reflection

- How did you know to make a short pause here?
- How did you know to make full stop?
- Did you have any trouble knowing where to make a short pause or full stop as you read?
- Was your pausing too short, too long, or just right?

Validating and Confirming

- Good—you made a full stop.
- I like the way you made a short pause/full stop here.
- I like the way you used the _____ punctuation mark to help you make a short pause/full stop here.

© 2009 Newmark Learning, LLC   Fluency Mini-Lessons • Grade 1   13

Pausing: Full Stop

Objectives

Students will:

- utilize punctuation to signal full stops while reading

- demonstrate understanding of the text through purposeful pausing

- use effective pausing to make their reading sound like talking

Mini-Lesson BLM 5, page 40

Knock-Knock Jokes

Reader 1: Knock, knock.
Reader 2: Who's there?
Reader 1: Ben.
Reader 2: Ben who?
Reader 1: Ben knocking on the door all afternoon!

Reader 1: Knock, knock.
Reader 2: Who's there?
Reader 1: Isadore.
Reader 2: Isadore who?
Reader 1: Isadore made out of wood?

Reader 1: Knock, knock.
Reader 2: Who's there?
Reader 1: Norma Lee.
Reader 2: Norma Lee who?
Reader 1: Norma Lee I'd use the doorbell, but it's broken!

Anchor Chart

Pausing

- We do not run all our words together.

- We pause, or rest, between some words.

- Pausing divides sentences into meaningful parts.

- Pausing makes our reading easier to understand.

- Punctuation helps us figure out when to pause.

- Punctuation helps us figure out how long to pause.

Introduce the Skill (10 minutes)

- **Say:** *We have learned that we do not run all our words together when reading. Instead, we pause, or rest, between some words. Pausing helps us divide our sentences into meaningful parts. Pausing helps our listeners understand what we are saying, too. Punctuation helps us figure out when to pause. The punctuation at the end of a sentence signals a longer pause than the punctuation inside the sentence. We come to a full stop and take a breath before beginning the next sentence.*

- Display a transparency of the fluency mini-lesson passage BLM on the overhead and read the title. **Say:** *These are knock-knock jokes. The author uses periods, question marks, and exclamation points to show us when to come to a full stop. Coming to a full stop helps the jokes sound right and make sense.*

- Have students listen and follow along as you read the jokes aloud, coming to a full stop at each period, question mark, and exclamation point. Then **say:** *Now I will read the first knock-knock joke without pausing. Listen closely.* Read the entire joke in a word-by-word manner without coming to a full stop at the periods, question marks, and exclamation point.

- **Ask:** *Which way is easiest to understand? Why?*

- Reread the class Anchor Chart together to remind students how good readers use pausing. (See the example provided.)

Group Guided Practice (15 minutes)

- Distribute the BLM for *Knock-Knock Jokes*. Ask students to choral-read the jokes with you one or more times. Next, allow the group to choral-read the jokes without your assistance.

- Distribute the Fluency Self-Assessment Master Checklist BLM from page 52. Then review the assessment criteria for pausing and integration (see the checklist, right). Ask students to give a thumbs-up or thumbs-down on each question based on the group's choral-reading. Discuss their responses.

- Pair students and ask them to read *Knock-Knock Jokes* together one or more times, alternating lines.

- Ask students to rate themselves on specific fluency skills covered in this lesson using their master checklists.

- Check comprehension by asking student partners to discuss the following: *What word does Ben's name stand for?* (been) *What phrase does Isadore's name stand for? (Is the door) What word does Norma Lee's name stand for?* (normally)

Individual/Partner Practice (15 minutes)

- Ask students to practice their oral reading skills by reading texts at their independent reading levels. You may want to use the leveled passages in Newmark Learning's Independent Fluency Practice Series.

- Carefully monitor students' progress, using the appropriate prompts (provided in the sidebar, right) to support their oral reading.

- Remind students to use the Self-Assessment Checklist to rate their oral reading skills and note any areas they might need to work on.

Performance (5 minutes)

- Invite individuals or partners to read a sentence or two from their fluency practice texts aloud for the class, paying special attention to pausing.

Self-Assessment Checklist

Pausing

☐ Did I pause to keep from running all my words together?

☐ Did I pause in the correct locations?

☐ Did I pause for the appropriate length of time?

☐ Did I pause to help my reading make sense?

☐ Did I use punctuation to help me figure out when to pause?

Integration

☐ Did I read the words right?

☐ Did I read the words at the right speed?

☐ Did I read with expression?

☐ Did my reading sound like talking?

☐ Did I understand what I read?

Pausing Prompts

Goal Oriented

- Listen to me read this. Can you hear me take a little breath at the comma (semicolon, dash, colon, ellipsis)?
- The period (question mark, exclamation point) means your voice makes a full stop.
- When I make a short pause, I don't stop completely and break the flow of my reading.
- When I finish a sentence, I make a full stop before continuing my reading.
- Notice what I do when I see a(n) comma (semicolon, dash, colon, ellipsis). My reading pauses briefly and then continues to help make ideas clear as I read.
- Notice what I do when I see a(n) period (question mark, exclamation point). My reading pauses with a full stop to show that I've read a complete sentence or idea.

Directive and Corrective Feedback

- Make a full stop at the period (question mark, exclamation point).
- Take a little breath when you see a(n) comma (semicolon, dash, colon, ellipsis).
- Read it like this with a short pause between the words.
- Read it like this with a full stop after the word.

Self-Monitoring and Reflection

- How did you know to make a short pause here?
- How did you know to make full stop?
- Did you have any trouble knowing where to make a short pause or full stop as you read?
- Was your pausing too short, too long, or just right?

•Validating and Confirming

- Good—you made a full stop.
- I like the way you made a short pause/full stop here.
- I like the way you used the _____ punctuation mark to help you make a short pause/full stop here!

Pausing: Text Structure and Organization

Objectives

Students will:
- utilize text structure and organization to signal pauses while reading
- demonstrate understanding of the text through purposeful pausing
- use effective pausing to make their reading sound like talking

Mini-Lesson BLM 6, page 41

Little Boy Blue

Little Boy Blue

Come blow your horn.

The sheep's in the meadow

The cow's in the corn.

And where is the boy who looks after the sheep?

He's under the haystack, fast asleep.

Anchor Chart

Pausing
- We do not run all our words together.
- We pause, or rest, between some words.
- Pausing divides sentences into meaningful parts.
- Pausing makes our reading easier to understand.
- Punctuation helps us figure out when to pause.
- Punctuation helps us figure out how long to pause.

Introduce the Skill (10 minutes)

- **Say:** *We have learned that we do not run all our words together when reading. Instead, we pause, or rest, between some words. Pausing helps us divide our sentences into meaningful parts. Pausing also helps our listeners understand what we are saying. Punctuation helps us figure out when to pause. Text structure and organization can help us figure out when to pause, too. One kind of text structure is a rhyming poem. We often pause and take a little breath at the end of each line in a rhyming poem.*

- Display a transparency of the fluency mini-lesson passage BLM on the overhead and read the title. **Say:** *This is a nursery rhyme. A nursery rhyme is one kind of rhyming poem. I will make a short pause at the end of each line to help the poem sound right and make sense. I will also watch for punctuation that signals short pauses and full stops.*

- Have students listen and follow along as you read the poem aloud, pausing briefly at the end of each line and appropriately at each punctuation mark. Then **say:** *I will read the nursery rhyme again. This time I won't pause. Listen closely.* Read the entire poem in a word-by-word manner without pausing.

- **Ask:** *Which way sounds better? Which way is easiest to understand? Why?*

- Reread the class Anchor Chart together to remind students how good readers use pausing. (See the example provided.) Then invite students to help you add one more entry on the chart: Text structure and organization can help us figure out when to pause.

Group Guided Practice (15 minutes)

- Distribute the BLM for *Little Boy Blue*. Ask students to echo-read each line, and then have them choral-read the nursery rhyme with you. Next, allow the group to choral-read the poem without your assistance.

- Distribute the Fluency Self-Assessment Master Checklist BLM from page 52. Then review the assessment criteria for pausing and integration (see the checklist, right). Ask students to give a thumbs-up or thumbs-down on each question based on the group's choral-reading. Then ask if they also used the structure of the poem to help them figure out when to pause. Discuss their responses.

- Pair students and ask them to read *Little Boy Blue* together one or more times, alternating lines.

- Ask students to rate themselves on specific fluency skills covered in this lesson using their master checklists.

- Check comprehension by asking student partners to discuss the following: *Who is Little Boy Blue? What is his job? Is he doing his job? Why or why not?*

Individual/Partner Practice (15 minutes)

- Ask students to practice their oral reading skills by reading texts at their independent reading levels. You may want to use the leveled passages in Newmark Learning's Independent Fluency Practice Series.

- Carefully monitor students' progress, using the appropriate prompts (provided in the sidebar, right) to support their oral reading.

- Remind students to use the Self-Assessment Checklist to rate their oral reading skills and note any areas they might need to work on.

Performance (5 minutes)

- Invite individuals or partners to read a sentence or two from their fluency practice texts aloud for the class, paying special attention to pausing.

Self-Assessment Checklist

Pausing
- ☐ Did I pause to keep from running all my words together?
- ☐ Did I pause in the correct locations?
- ☐ Did I pause for the appropriate length of time?
- ☐ Did I pause to help my reading make sense?
- ☐ Did I use punctuation to help me figure out when to pause?

Integration
- ☐ Did I read the words right?
- ☐ Did I read the words at the right speed?
- ☐ Did I read with expression?
- ☐ Did my reading sound like talking?
- ☐ Did I understand what I read?

Pausing Prompts

Goal Oriented
- Listen to me read this. Can you hear me take a little breath at the comma (semicolon, dash, colon, ellipsis)?
- The period (question mark, exclamation point) means your voice makes a full stop.
- When I make a short pause, I don't stop completely and break the flow of my reading.
- When I finish a sentence, I make a full stop before continuing my reading.
- Notice what I do when I see a(n) comma (semicolon, dash, colon, ellipsis). My reading pauses briefly and then continues to help make ideas clear as I read.
- Notice what I do when I see a(n) period (question mark, exclamation point). My reading pauses with a full stop to show that I've read a complete sentence or idea.

Directive and Corrective Feedback
- Make a full stop at the period (question mark, exclamation point).
- Take a little breath when you see a(n) comma (semicolon, dash, colon, ellipsis).
- Read it like this with a short pause between the words.
- Read it like this with a full stop after the word.

Self-Monitoring and Reflection
- How did you know to make a short pause here?
- How did you know to make full stop?
- Did you have any trouble knowing where to make a short pause or full stop as you read?
- Was your pausing too short, too long, or just right?

Validating and Confirming.
- Good—you made a full stop.
- I like the way you made a short pause/full stop here.
- I like the way you used the _____ punctuation mark to help you make a short pause/full stop here.

Inflection/Intonation: Pitch

Objectives

Students will:

- make their voices rise at a question mark and fall at a period

- demonstrate understanding of the text through purposeful inflection and intonation

- use effective inflection and intonation to make their reading sound like talking

---

Mini-Lesson BLM 7, page 42

Student Interview

Teacher: What's your favorite animal?
Student: I like my dog. He's a Chocolate Lab named Brownie.
Teacher: What's your favorite pair of shoes?
Student: I like my brown shoes. They're the color of chocolate.
Teacher: What's your favorite part of school?
Student: I like lunchtime. Sometimes my mom packs a chocolate bar in my lunch box.
Teacher: I think I know the answer to the next question. What's your favorite flavor of ice cream?
Student: I like vanilla. Surprise!

Anchor Chart

Inflection/Intonation

- We do not read every word the same.
- We read some words louder and some words softer. This is called volume.
- We emphasize some words. This is called stress.
- We read some words higher and some words lower. This is called pitch.
- Ending punctuation helps us know when to make our voices rise or fall.
- Changing the way we read words helps our reading sound like talking.

Introduce the Skill (10 minutes)

- **Say:** *When we talk, we do not say every word the same. Instead, we use different kinds of inflection and intonation. We say some words louder and some words softer. This is called volume. We emphasize some words. This is called stress. We also say some words at a higher pitch* (model by making your voice rise) *and some words at a lower pitch* (model by making your voice fall). *In reading, the ending punctuation helps us figure out when to use a higher or lower pitch. We make our voices rise when we see a question mark. We make our voices fall when we see a period. When we see an exclamation point, our voices may rise or fall depending on what we are reading.*

- Display a transparency of the fluency mini-lesson passage BLM on the overhead and read the title. **Say:** *This is an interview. The author uses question marks, periods, and exclamation points to show us when to make our voices rise and fall. Changing our pitch at each question mark, period, and exclamation point helps the sentences sound right and make sense. Changing our pitch makes our reading sound like talking.*

- Have students listen and follow along as you read the interview aloud, making your voice rise at each question mark and fall at each period. Stop to experiment with a rising and falling pitch at the exclamation point and invite students to tell you which sounds better (a rising pitch). Then **say:** *Now I will read the interview without making my voice rise and fall. Listen closely.* Read the entire interview in a monotone.

- **Ask:** *Which way sounds the best? Which way is easiest to understand? Why?*

- Invite students to help you create a class Anchor Chart to remind them how good readers use inflection and intonation. (See the example provided.) When you are finished, ask students to echo-read the entire chart. Then post the chart in the classroom for future reference.

Group Guided Practice (15 minutes)

- Distribute the BLM for *Student Interview*. Divide students into two groups and ask them to choral-read the interview with you one or more times. Next, allow the groups to choral-read their parts without your assistance.

- Distribute the Fluency Self-Assessment Master Checklist BLM from page 52. Then review the assessment criteria for inflection/intonation and integration (see the checklist, right). Ask students to give a thumbs-up or thumbs-down on each question based on the group's choral-reading. Discuss their responses.

- Pair students and ask them to read *Student Interview* together one or more times.

- Ask students to rate themselves on specific fluency skills covered in this lesson using their master checklists.

- Check comprehension by asking student partners to discuss the following: *Why did the student say "Surprise!" at the end? How would you answer each interview question?*

Individual/Partner Practice (15 minutes)

- Ask students to practice their oral reading skills by reading texts at their independent reading levels. You may want to use the leveled passages in Newmark Learning's Independent Fluency Practice Series.

- Carefully monitor students' progress, using the appropriate prompts (provided in the sidebar, right) to support their oral reading.

- Remind students to use the Self-Assessment Checklist to rate their oral reading skills and note any areas they might need to work on.

Performance (5 minutes)

- Invite individuals or partners to read a sentence or two from their fluency practice texts aloud for the class, paying special attention to inflection and intonation.

Self-Assessment Checklist

Inflection/Intonation
- [ ] Did I make my voice rise at a question mark?
- [ ] Did I make my voice fall at a period?
- [ ] Did I think about what the author was saying so I would know when to read louder or softer?
- [ ] Did I think about what the author was saying so I would know when to stress words?

Integration
- [ ] Did I read the words right?
- [ ] Did I read the words at the right speed?
- [ ] Did I read with expression?
- [ ] Did my reading sound like talking?
- [ ] Did I understand what I read?

Inflection/Intonation Prompts

Goal Oriented
- Listen to how I read this. Can you hear my voice go down at the period?
- Listen to how I read this. Can you hear my voice go up at the question mark?
- Listen to how my voice gets louder.
- Listen to how my voice gets softer.
- Emphasize the word _____ like this.
- Notice what I do when I read the bold print (italicized words, words in all uppercase letters).

Directive and Corrective Feedback
- Make your voice go down at the period.
- Make your voice go up at the question mark.
- Read it louder.
- Read it softer.
- Stress the word _____ in this sentence.
- Watch for bold print (italicized words, words in all uppercase letters). Emphasize those words.

Self-Monitoring and Reflection
- What should your voice do when you see a period?
- What should your voice do when you see a question mark?
- Should your voice go up or down at this exclamation point?
- How did you know to read louder?
- How did you know to read softer?
- What made you emphasize the word _____?

Validating and Confirming
- Good job at making your voice rise and fall.
- You read that part louder/softer—way to think like the author!
- You stressed exactly the right words in that sentence. Good thinking!

Inflection/Intonation: Volume

Objectives

Students will:

- use a higher or lower volume to reflect what the author or characters are saying

- demonstrate understanding of the text through purposeful inflection and intonation

- use effective inflection and intonation to make their reading sound like talking

Mini-Lesson BLM 8, page 43

The Hungry Fox

Fox went to the farm. He wanted to eat Rooster.

Cow got up. "Shoo, Fox, shoo!" said Cow. "Go away! Come back some other day."

Sheep got up. "Shoo, Fox, shoo!" said Sheep. "Go away! Come back some other day."

Pig got up. "Shoo, Fox, shoo!" said Pig. "Go away! Come back some other day."

Rooster got up. "Cock-a-doodle-doo!" said Rooster.

The farmer got up. "Shoo, Fox, shoo!" said the farmer. "Go away, and do NOT come back some other day!"

Anchor Chart

Inflection/Intonation

- We do not read every word the same.

- We read some words louder and some words softer. This is called volume.

- We emphasize some words. This is called stress.

- We read some words higher and some words lower. This is called pitch.

- Ending punctuation helps us know when to make our voices rise or fall.

- Changing the way we read words helps our reading sound like talking.

Introduce the Skill (10 minutes)

- **Say:** *We have learned that we use different kinds of inflection and intonation when we read. We say some words higher and some words lower. This is called pitch. We emphasize some words. This is called stress. We also say some words at a louder volume* (model with your voice) *and some words at a softer volume* (model with your voice). *We pay close attention to what the author or characters are saying to help us figure out when to use a louder or softer volume. For example, how would we read if the author is saying something exciting or a character is calling out?* (loud) *How would we read if the author is saying something sad or a character is sneaking around?* (soft)

- Display a transparency of the fluency mini-lesson passage BLM on the overhead and read the title. **Say:** *This is a story about a fox. At first, the fox is sneaking onto a farm, so I will read at a soft volume. Then the animals begin calling out to the fox. I will read the animals' words at a louder volume, especially where I see exclamation points. Changing my volume helps the story sound right and make sense. Changing my volume makes my reading sound like talking, too.*

- Have students listen and follow along as you read the story aloud, using a softer and louder volume as described above. Then **say:** *Now I will read the story at the same volume all the way through. Listen closely.* Read the entire story in a monotone.

- **Ask:** *Which way sounds the best? Which way is easiest to understand? Why?*

- Reread the class Anchor Chart together to remind students how good readers use inflection and intonation. (See the example provided.)

Group Guided Practice (15 minutes)

- Distribute the BLM for *The Hungry Fox*. Invite students to choral-read the story with you one or more times. Next, allow the group to choral-read the story without your assistance.

- Distribute the Fluency Self-Assessment Master Checklist BLM from page 52. Then review the assessment criteria for inflection/intonation and integration (see the checklist, right). Ask students to give a thumbs-up or thumbs-down on each question based on the group's choral-reading. Discuss their responses.

- Pair students and ask them to read *The Hungry Fox* together one or more times.

- Ask students to rate themselves on specific fluency skills covered in this lesson using their master checklists.

- Check comprehension by asking students to summarize or retell the story to a partner.

MODEL SUMMARY

A fox went to a farm to eat a rooster. The farm animals told the fox to go away and come back some other day. Then the rooster woke up the farmer. The farmer told the fox NOT to come back.

Individual/Partner Practice (15 minutes)

- Ask students to practice their oral reading skills by reading texts at their independent reading levels. You may want to use the leveled passages in Newmark Learning's Independent Fluency Practice Series.

- Carefully monitor students' progress, using the appropriate prompts (provided in the sidebar, right) to support their oral reading.

- Remind students to use the Self-Assessment Checklist to rate their oral reading skills and note any areas they might need to work on.

Performance (5 minutes)

- Invite individuals or partners to read a sentence or two from their fluency practice texts aloud for the class, paying special attention to inflection and intonation.

Self-Assessment Checklist

Inflection/Intonation

☐ Did I make my voice rise at a question mark?

☐ Did I make my voice fall at a period?

☐ Did I think about what the author was saying so I would know when to read louder or softer?

☐ Did I think about what the author was saying so I would know when to stress words?

Integration

☐ Did I read the words right?

☐ Did I read the words at the right speed?

☐ Did I read with expression?

☐ Did my reading sound like talking?

☐ Did I understand what I read?

Inflection/Intonation Prompts

Goal Oriented

- Listen to how I read this. Can you hear my voice go down at the period?
- Listen to how I read this. Can you hear my voice go up at the question mark?
- Listen to how my voice gets louder.
- Listen to how my voice gets softer.
- Emphasize the word _____ like this.
- Notice what I do when I read the bold print (italicized words, words in all uppercase letters).

Directive and Corrective Feedback

- Make your voice go down at the period.
- Make your voice go up at the question mark.
- Read it louder.
- Read it softer.
- Stress the word _____ in this sentence.
- Watch for bold print (italicized words, words in all uppercase letters). Emphasize those words.

Self-Monitoring and Reflection

- What should your voice do when you see a period?
- What should your voice do when you see a question mark?
- Should your voice go up or down at this exclamation point?
- How did you know to read louder?
- How did you know to read softer?
- What made you emphasize the word _____?

Validating and Confirming

- Good job at making your voice rise and fall.
- You read that part louder/softer—way to think like the author!
- You stressed exactly the right words in that sentence. Good thinking!

Inflection/Intonation: Stress

Objectives

Students will:

- stress particular words to emphasize meaning and reflect the language patterns of the text

- demonstrate understanding of the text through purposeful inflection and intonation

- use effective inflection and intonation to make their reading sound like talking

Mini-Lesson BLM 9, page 44

Tiny Tim

I had a little puppy.
His name was Tiny Tim.
I put him in the bathtub
To see if he could swim.

He drank up all the water.
He ate a bar of soap.
The next thing I knew,
He had a bubble in his throat.

In came the doctor,
In came the nurse,
In came the lady with the alligator purse.

"Mumps!" said the doctor.
"Measles!" said the nurse.
"Hiccups!" said the lady with the alligator purse.

Out went the doctor.
Out went the nurse.
Out went the lady with the alligator purse.

Anchor Chart

Inflection/Intonation

- We do not read every word the same.

- We read some words louder and some words softer. This is called volume.

- We emphasize some words. This is called stress.

- We read some words higher and some words lower. This is called pitch.

- Ending punctuation helps us know when to make our voices rise or fall.

- Changing the way we read words helps our reading sound like talking.

Introduce the Skill (10 minutes)

- **Say:** *We have learned that we use different kinds of inflection and intonation when we read. We say some words louder and some words softer. This is called volume. We say some words higher and some words lower. This is called pitch. We also emphasize some words. This is called stress. Sometimes words we need to stress are in boldfaced letters, italic letters, or all uppercase letters. We also pay close attention to what the author or characters are saying to help us figure out when to stress particular words. We think about the language patterns of the text, too. For example, we stress certain words in a joke to make it funnier, or we stress certain words in a song or poem to keep the rhythm going.*

- Display a transparency of the fluency mini-lesson passage BLM on the overhead and read the title. **Say:** *This is a jump-rope rhyme about a puppy. In the first two verses, I need to stress an important word in each line to keep the rhythm going.* (had, name, put, see / drank, ate, next, bubble). *In the last three verses, I need to stress the first word in each line to keep the rhythm going. The lines in the third and fifth verse begin with "In" or "Out," so they're also signaling to a new jumper when to join and leave. Stressing these words helps the rhyme sound right and make sense.*

- Have students listen and follow along as you read the jump-rope rhyme aloud, underlining and stressing the words as described above. Then **say:** *Now I will read all the words in the rhyme the same way. Listen closely. Read the entire rhyme in a monotone.*

- **Ask:** *Which way sounds the best? Which way is easiest to understand? Why?*

- Reread the class Anchor Chart together to remind students how good readers use inflection and intonation. (See the example provided.)

Group Guided Practice (15 minutes)

- Distribute the BLM for *Tiny Tim*. Help students underline the words to stress. Ask them to echo-read each line, and then have them choral-read the rhyme with you. Next, allow the group to choral-read the rhyme without your assistance.

- Distribute the Fluency Self-Assessment Master Checklist BLM from page 52. Then review the assessment criteria for inflection/intonation and integration (see the checklist, right). Ask students to give a thumbs-up or thumbs-down on each question based on the group's choral-reading. Discuss their responses.

- Pair students and ask them to read *Tiny Tim* together one or more times, alternating lines.

- Ask students to rate themselves on specific fluency skills covered in this lesson using their master checklists.

- Check comprehension by asking student partners to discuss the following: *Who was Tiny Tim? What did Tiny Tim do? Who came to help?*

Individual/Partner Practice (15 minutes)

- Ask students to practice their oral reading skills by reading texts at their independent reading levels. You may want to use the leveled passages in Newmark Learning's Independent Fluency Practice Series.

- Carefully monitor students' progress, using the appropriate prompts (provided in the sidebar, right) to support their oral reading.

- Remind students to use the Self-Assessment Checklist to rate their oral reading skills and note any areas they might need to work on.

Performance (5 minutes)

- Invite individuals or partners to read a sentence or two from their fluency practice texts aloud for the class, paying special attention to inflection and intonation.

Self-Assessment Checklist

Inflection/Intonation

☐ Did I make my voice rise at a question mark?
☐ Did I make my voice fall at a period?
☐ Did I think about what the author was saying so I would know when to read louder or softer?
☐ Did I think about what the author was saying so I would know when to stress words?

Integration

☐ Did I read the words right?
☐ Did I read the words at the right speed?
☐ Did I read with expression?
☐ Did my reading sound like talking?
☐ Did I understand what I read?

Inflection/Intonation Prompts

Goal Oriented
- Listen to how I read this. Can you hear my voice go down at the period?
- Listen to how I read this. Can you hear my voice go up at the question mark?
- Listen to how my voice gets louder.
- Listen to how my voice gets softer.
- Emphasize the word _____ like this.
- Notice what I do when I read the bold print (italicized words, words in all uppercase letters).

Directive and Corrective Feedback
- Make your voice go down at the period.
- Make your voice go up at the question mark.
- Read it louder.
- Read it softer.
- Stress the word _____ in this sentence.
- Watch for bold print (italicized words, words in all uppercase letters). Emphasize those words.

Self-Monitoring and Reflection
- What should your voice do when you see a period?
- What should your voice do when you see a question mark?
- Should your voice go up or down at this exclamation point?
- How did you know to read louder?
- How did you know to read softer?
- What made you emphasize the word _____?

Validating and Confirming
- Good job at making your voice rise and fall.
- You read that part louder/softer—way to think like the author!
- You stressed exactly the right words in that sentence. Good thinking!

Phrasing: High-Frequency Word Phrases

Objectives

Students will:
- read short word groups and sentences as complete phrases
- demonstrate understanding of the text through purposeful phrasing
- use effective phrasing to make their reading sound like talking

---

Mini-Lesson BLM 10, page 45

Bus Trip

Group 1: Look for some people.
Group 2: How many people?
Group 1: A number of people.
Group 2: What will they do?
Group 1: Get on the bus.
Group 2: Could you go? You and I?
Group 1: We will go. Now is the time.
Group 2: We will go. From here to there.
Group 1 and **Group 2:** This is a good day!

Anchor Chart

Phrasing

- Phrases are groups of words.
- Phrases contain two or more words.
- We read all the words together.
- Reading a phrase should sound like talking.
- Think about what the words in the phrase mean when they are together.

Introduce the Skill (10 minutes)

- **Say:** *Sometimes we read groups of words together. Groups of words that go together are called phrases. Sometimes two words can be a phrase. Sometimes three or more words can be a phrase. Sometimes a whole sentence can be a phrase. We read the words in a phrase together. The words sound right together. The words make sense together, too. When you read a phrase, your reading should sound like talking. Reading without your finger helps you phrase the words together.*

- Display a transparency of the fluency mini-lesson passage BLM on the overhead and read the title. **Say:** *This whole story is made of words we are learning to recognize very quickly. The whole story is made of phrases, too. I will read each group of words as a phrase. Remember—the words in a phrase go together.*

- Have students listen and follow along as you read the passage aloud, treating each group of words as a connected phrase. Then **say:** *I will read the story again. This time, some of the groups of words will not sound like phrases. Listen closely. Put your hand on your head if you hear a group of words that does not sound like a phrase.* Go through the passage again, reading some of the parts in a staccato, word-by-word manner. Watch to see which students respond to your lack of phrasing.

- **Ask:** *Which groups of words did not sound like phrases? Why?*

- Invite students to help you create a class Anchor Chart to remind them how good readers read phrases. (See the example provided.) When you are finished, ask students to echo-read the entire chart. Then post the chart in the classroom for future reference.

Group Guided Practice (15 minutes)

- Distribute the BLM for *Bus Trip*. Divide students into Group 1 and Group 2 and ask them to choral-read their parts with you one or more times. Next, allow the groups to choral-read their parts without your assistance.

- Distribute the Fluency Self-Assessment Master Checklist BLM from page 52. Then review the assessment criteria for phrasing and integration (see the checklist, right). Ask students to give a thumbs-up or thumbs-down on each question based on the group's choral read. Discuss their responses.

- Pair students, and then put two pairs together. Assign one pair as Group 1 and one pair as Group 2, and invite them to read *Bus Trip* together one or more times.

- Ask students to rate themselves on specific fluency skills covered in this lesson using their master checklists.

- Check comprehension by asking students to summarize or retell the story to a partner.

MODEL SUMMARY

Some kids looked for people. The people were supposed to go on a bus trip. Then the kids decided to go on the bus trip, too. They had a good day.

Individual/Partner Practice (15 minutes)

- Ask students to practice their oral reading skills by reading texts at their independent reading levels. You may want to use the leveled passages in Newmark Learning's Independent Fluency Practice Series.

- Carefully monitor students' progress, using the appropriate prompts (provided in the sidebar, right) to support students' oral reading progress.

- Remind students to use the Self-Assessment Checklist to rate their oral reading skills and note any areas they might need to work on.

Performance (5 minutes)

- Invite individuals or partners to read a sentence or two from their fluency practice texts aloud for the class, paying special attention to phrasing.

Self-Assessment Checklist

Phrasing

☐ Did I notice the phrases?

☐ Did I read all the words in each phrase together?

☐ Did I think about what the words in the phrase mean when they are together?

Integration

☐ Did I read the words right?

☐ Did I read the words at the right speed?

☐ Did I read with expression?

☐ Did my reading sound like talking?

☐ Did I understand what I read?

Phrasing Prompts

Goal Oriented
- Listen to how reading sounds like talking.
- Listen to how I group words together into phrases.
- Read it like this: _____.
- These words make sense together. Listen to how I read the words.
- Watch how I read the words without using my finger.
- Phrasing is not choppy reading like this:
  Look . . . for . . . some . . . people.

Directive and Corrective Feedback
- Now read the text just like I did.
- Repeat after me and make your reading sound like mine.
- Read the words _____ together as a group.
- Put your words together so that it sounds like talking.
- Read this much all together. (Cover part of the text.)
- Try that again and put the words together.
- Try reading with your eyes and not your finger.

Self-Monitoring and Reflection
- How did you make your reading sound like talking?
- What did you notice that made you group your words together?
- How did you know to put the words _____ together?
- How did grouping the words _____ together help you understand what you read?
- I noticed you stopped pointing with your finger. Did your eyes have any trouble keeping their place?
- Was your reading smooth or choppy?

Validating and Confirming
- I noticed that you put the words _____ together as a group. That makes your reading sound like talking.
- You put your words together. Good!

Phrasing: Subject/Predicate Phrases

Objectives

Students will:

- read subjects and predicates as complete phrases
- demonstrate understanding of the text through purposeful phrasing
- use effective phrasing to make their reading sound like talking

Mini-Lesson BLM 11, page 46

Silly Zoo

The bear had no hair.
The cubs sat in tubs.
The cow took a bow.
The goat wore a coat.

The deer gave a cheer.
The seal wasn't real.
The fish made a wish.
The bat wore a hat.

The snake liked to bake.
The birds said long words.
The lion was cryin',
But the giraffe . . . had to laugh!

Anchor Chart

Phrasing

- Phrases are groups of words.
- Phrases contain two or more words.
- We read all the words together.
- Reading a phrase should sound like talking.
- Think about what the words in the phrase mean when they are together.

Introduce the Skill (10 minutes)

- **Say:** *We have learned that we sometimes read two or more words together. Groups of words that go together are called phrases. Reading in phrases sounds like talking. Reading in phrases helps us understand what we are reading, too.*

- Display a transparency of the fluency mini-lesson passage BLM on the overhead and read the title. **Say:** *We often divide sentences into phrases. I will divide the sentences in this poem into phrases. The first phrase will tell what the sentence is about, or the subject. The second phrase will tell what the subject does. Remember—the words in a phrase go together.*

- Have students listen and follow along as you read the poem aloud. Pause briefly and draw a slash mark on the transparency between each subject and predicate. (The bear / had no hair.) Then **say:** *I will read the poem again. This time, some of the groups of words will not sound like they go together. Listen closely. Put your hand on your head if you hear some words that don't sound like they go together.* Read the poem again, dividing some of the sentences into awkward phrases. (The bear had / no hair.) Watch to see which students respond to the incorrect phrasing.

- **Ask:** *Which groups of words did not sound like good phrases? Why?*

- Reread the class Anchor Chart together to remind students how good readers read phrases. (See the example provided.)

Group Guided Practice (15 minutes)

- Distribute the BLM for *Silly Zoo*. Help students add slash marks to divide each sentence between the subject and predicate, and then invite them to choral-read the poem with you one or more times. Next, allow the group to choral-read the poem without your assistance.

- Distribute the Fluency Self-Assessment Master Checklist BLM from page 52. Then review the assessment criteria for phrasing and integration (see the checklist, right). Ask students to give a thumbs-up or thumbs-down on each question based on the group's choral-reading. Discuss their responses.

- Pair students and invite them to read *Silly Zoo* together one or more times, alternating lines.

- Ask students to rate themselves on specific fluency skills covered in this lesson using their master checklists.

• Check comprehension by asking students to tell their partner why the author titled the poem *Silly Zoo*. Then have them tell which animal they think is the silliest and why.

Individual/Partner Practice (15 minutes)

• Ask students to practice their oral reading skills by reading texts at their independent reading levels. You may want to use the leveled passages in Newmark Learning's Independent Fluency Practice Series.

• Carefully monitor students' progress, using the appropriate prompts (provided in the sidebar, right) to support their oral reading.

• Remind students to use the Self-Assessment Checklist to rate their oral reading skills and note any areas they might need to work on.

Performance (5 minutes)

• Invite individuals or partners to read a sentence or two from their fluency practice texts aloud for the class, paying special attention to phrasing.

Self-Assessment Checklist

Phrasing

☐ Did I notice the phrases?

☐ Did I read all the words in each phrase together?

☐ Did I think about what the words in the phrase mean when they are together?

Integration

☐ Did I read the words right?

☐ Did I read the words at the right speed?

☐ Did I read with expression?

☐ Did my reading sound like talking?

☐ Did I understand what I read?

Phrasing Prompts

Goal Oriented

• Listen to how reading sounds like talking.
• Listen to how I group words together into phrases.
• Read it like this _____.
• These words make sense together. Listen to how I read them.
• Watch how I read the words without using my finger.
• Phrasing is not choppy reading like this:
  Look . . . for . . . some . . . people.

Directive and Corrective Feedback

• Now read the text just like I did.
• Repeat after me and make your reading sound like mine.
• Read the words _____ together as a group.
• Put your words together so that it sounds like talking.
• Read this much all together. (Cover part of the text.)
• Try that again and put the words together.
• Try reading with your eyes and not your finger.

Self-Monitoring and Reflection

• How did you make your reading sound like talking?
• What did you notice that made you group your words together?
• How did you know to put the words _____ together?
• How did grouping the words _____ together help you understand what you read?
• I noticed you stopped pointing with your finger. Did your eyes have any trouble keeping their place?
• Was your reading smooth or choppy?

Validating and Confirming

• I noticed that you put the words _____ together as a group, that makes your reading sound like talking.
• You put your words together. Good!

Prepositional Phrases

Objectives

Students will:

- read the words in a prepositional phrase together
- demonstrate understanding of the text through purposeful phrasing
- use effective phrasing to make their reading sound like talking

---

Mini-Lesson BLM 12, page 47

How Many Puddles?

Juan counted puddles on the way to school.

"I see a puddle in my yard," said Juan. Juan walked through the first puddle.

"I see a puddle at the corner," said Juan. Juan skipped through the second puddle.

"I see a puddle by the fence," said Juan. Juan hopped through the third puddle.

"I see a puddle under the flagpole," said Juan. Juan ran through the fourth puddle.

Juan went into his classroom. "I saw four puddles on the way to school," he said.

"I see a puddle IN the school," said the teacher.

Juan looked down. Water dripped from his shoes.

"Oops!" said Juan. "That makes five puddles!"

Anchor Chart

Phrasing

- Phrases are groups of words.
- Phrases contain two or more words.
- We read all the words together.
- Reading a phrase should sound like talking.
- Think about what the words in the phrase mean when they are together.

Introduce the Skill (10 minutes)

- **Say:** *We have learned that we sometimes read two or more words together. Groups of words that go together are called phrases. Reading in phrases sounds like talking. Reading in phrases helps us understand what we are reading, too.*

- Display a transparency of the fluency mini-lesson passage BLM on the overhead and read the title. **Say:** *We often divide sentences into phrases. Some phrases begin with words called prepositions. Some prepositions you know are on, to, in, through, at, by, under, into, and from. Phrases with prepositions give us more information about something in the sentence. I will look for phrases with prepositions as I read this story. Remember—the words in a phrase go together.*

- Have students listen and follow along as you read the story aloud. Pause briefly and draw a slash before each prepositional phrase. (Juan counted puddles / on the way / to school.) Then **say:** *I will read the story again. This time, some of the groups of words will not sound like they go together. Listen closely. Put your hand on your head if you hear some words that don't sound like they go together.* Read the story again, dividing some of the sentences into awkward phrases. (Juan counted / puddles on / the way to / school.) Watch to see which students respond to the incorrect phrasing.

- **Ask:** *Which groups of words did not sound like good phrases? Why?*

- Reread the class Anchor Chart together to remind students how good readers read phrases. (See the example provided.)

Group Guided Practice (15 minutes)

- Distribute the BLM for *How Many Puddles?* Help students add slash marks before each prepositional phrase, and then invite them to choral-read the story with you one or more times. Next, allow the group to choral-read the story without your assistance.

- Distribute the Fluency Self-Assessment Master Checklist BLM from page 52. Then review the assessment criteria for phrasing and integration (see the checklist, right). Ask students to give a thumbs-up or thumbs-down on each question based on the group's choral-reading. Discuss their responses.

- Pair students and invite them to read *How Many Puddles?* together one or more times, alternating lines.

- Ask students to rate themselves on specific fluency skills covered in this lesson using their master checklists.

- Check comprehension by asking students to summarize or retell the story to a partner.

MODEL SUMMARY

Juan saw four puddles on the way to school. He walked, skipped, hopped, and ran through the puddles. His wet shoes made a new puddle in the classroom

Individual/Partner Practice (15 minutes)

- Ask students to practice their oral reading skills by reading texts at their independent reading levels. You may want to use the leveled passages in Newmark Learning's Independent Fluency Practice Series.

- Carefully monitor students' progress using the appropriate prompts (provided in the sidebar, right) to support their oral reading.

- Remind students to use the Self-Assessment Checklist to rate their oral reading skills and note any areas they might need to work on.

Performance (5 minutes)

- Invite individuals or partners to read a sentence or two from their fluency practice texts aloud for the class, paying special attention to phrasing.

Self-Assessment Checklist

Phrasing

☐ Did I notice the phrases?

☐ Did I read all the words in each phrase together?

☐ Did I think about what the words in the phrase mean when they are together?

Integration

☐ Did I read the words right?

☐ Did I read the words at the right speed?

☐ Did I read with expression?

☐ Did my reading sound like talking?

☐ Did I understand what I read?

Phrasing Prompts

Goal Oriented

- Listen to how reading sounds like talking.
- Listen to how I group words together into phrases.
- Read it like this _____.
- These words make sense together. Listen to how I read them.
- Watch how I read the words without using my finger.
- Phrasing is not choppy reading like this: Look . . . for . . . some . . . people.

Directive and Corrective Feedback

- Now read the text just like I did.
- Repeat after me and make your reading sound like mine.
- Read the words _____ together as a group.
- Put your words together so that it sounds like talking.
- Read this much all together. (Cover part of the text.)
- Try that again and put the words together.
- Try reading with your eyes and not your finger.

Self-Monitoring and Reflection

- How did you make your reading sound like talking?
- What did you notice that made you group your words together?
- How did you know to put the words _____ together?
- How did grouping the words _____ together help you understand what you read?
- I noticed you stopped pointing with your finger. Did your eyes have any trouble keeping their place?
- Was your reading smooth or choppy?

Validating and Confirming

- I noticed that you put the words _____ together as a group, that makes your reading sound like talking.
- You put your words together. Good!

Expression: Anticipation and Mood

Objectives

Students will:

- use the title and other text and graphic clues to anticipate the mood of a reading selection
- match their tone of voice to the intended mood
- demonstrate understanding of the text through purposeful expression
- use effective expression to make their reading sound like talking

Mini-Lesson BLM 13, page 48

Treasure Island?

An island is land with water all the way around it. Ships go by the island.

Sometimes things fall off the ships. The things float to the island. People find the things on the beach!

One island in the North Sea is call Terschelling (ter-SKEL-ing). People may soon call it Treasure Island, though. Strange things are always floating to this island!

One time, people found lots of sweaters on the beach. Another time, they found lots of tennis shoes. Another time they found lots of children's toys.

Yesterday, a ship was in a storm. Lots of bananas fell off the ship. People found the bananas on the beach.

The people talked about the bananas. "They might be a little salty!" some people said.

What will the people do with all those bananas? "We could send them to a zoo!" said one man on the beach.

Anchor Chart

Expression

- We do not use the same tone of voice for everything we read.
- Our tone of voice should match the mood of the passage.
- We can figure out, or anticipate, the mood from the title and other clues.
- We use the author's or charac ters' words to confirm their feelings.
- Reading with expression helps the passage sound right and make sense.
- We use pacing, pausing, inflection/intonation, and phrasing to read with expression.

Introduce the Skill (10 minutes)

- **Say:** *People use many different tones of voice. What tone of voice would you use to tell about a sick pet?* (sad) *What tone would you use to tell about a silly movie?* (happy) *The tone we use shows our mood. People can figure out, or anticipate, our mood from clues such as the look on our face, what we are doing with our hands, or how we are standing or sitting. When they hear our voice, they confirm how we are feeling. Authors use mood in their writing, too. Readers can guess what mood the author is using from clues such as the title, pictures, bold print, or punctuation. Then readers think about what the author or characters are saying to confirm their guesses. Reading in the correct mood helps the passage sound right and make sense.*

- Display a transparency of the fluency mini-lesson passage BLM and read the title. **Say:** *Many newspaper articles are serious, but I anticipate that this one will be funny. The title is unusual and has a question mark after it. I see exclamation points after some of the sentences. I will use a happy tone to read this news story. Then you can tell me whether the mood sounds right.*

- Have students listen and follow along as you read the article aloud in a lighthearted manner. Then ask students if they think your tone of voice fit the mood of the article. **Say:** *Now I will read the beginning of the article in some other ways. I will pretend the mood of the article is serious, then sad, then scary. Listen closely.* Read the first few paragraphs as described. **Ask:** *Which tone of voice sounds the best? Why?*

- Invite students to help you create a class Anchor Chart to remind them how good readers read with expression. (See the example provided.) Then ask students to echo-read the entire chart. Then post the chart in the classroom for future reference.

Group Guided Practice (15 minutes)

- Distribute the BLM for *Treasure Island?* Have students echo-read each sentence. Then have them choral-read the article with you. Next, have them choral-read the article without your assistance.

- Distribute the Fluency Self-Assessment Master Checklist BLM from page 52. Review the assessment criteria for expression and integration (see the checklist, right). Ask students to give a thumbs-up or thumbs-down on each question based on the group's choral-reading. Discuss their responses.

- Pair students and ask them to read *Treasure Island?* together one or more times.

- Ask students to rate themselves on specific fluency skills covered in this lesson using their master checklists.

- Check comprehension by asking students to summarize or retell the news article to a partner.

MODEL SUMMARY

A ship was in a storm. Bananas fell off the ship and floated to the beach of an island. The people on the island found the bananas. Now they are trying to decide what to do with them.

Individual/Partner Practice (15 minutes)

- Ask students to practice their oral reading skills by reading texts at their independent reading levels. You may want to use the leveled passages in Newmark Learning's Independent Fluency Practice Series.

- Carefully monitor students' progress, using the appropriate prompts (provided in the sidebar, right) to support their oral reading.

- Remind students to use the Self-Assessment Checklist to rate their oral reading skills and note any areas they might need to work on.

Performance (5 minutes)

- Invite individuals or partners to read a sentence or two from their fluency practice texts aloud for the class, paying special attention to reading with expression.

Self-Assessment Checklist

Expression

- ☐ Did I look for clues so I could anticipate the mood of the passage?
- ☐ Did I use my tone of voice, facial expressions, and body language to express what the author or characters were thinking or feeling?
- ☐ Did I change my reading when something new was about to happen?

Integration

- ☐ Did I read the words right?
- ☐ Did I read the words at the right speed?
- ☐ Did I read with expression?
- ☐ Did my reading sound like talking?
- ☐ Did I understand what I read?

Expression Prompts

Goal Oriented
- Let's read the title and look at the pictures. That will help us anticipate the mood of the passage.
- I see quotation marks, so the character is talking. I need to make my voice sound like the character's voice.
- I'll pretend to be that character. Listen to how I make my reading sound like he/she might talk.
- I need to make my voice, face, and body match what the author/character is saying when I read.
- Listen to me read this. Can you hear how excited (sad, proud, frightened) my voice sounds?

Directive and Corrective Feedback
- Make your voice sound excited (sad, proud, frightened).
- Make the character's voice match his/her actions and feelings.
- Read it like the author would say it.
- Repeat after me and read with expression.
- Use the punctuation to help you put expression in your voice.

Self-Monitoring and Reflection
- How did you know what tone of voice to use?
- Where did you read with good expression?
- What part do you need to read again with more expression?
- Did you use pacing (pausing, inflection/ intonation, phrasing) to help you read with expression?

Validating and Confirming
- You noticed the funny pictures, so you used a happy tone of voice. Good!
- You sounded excited (sad, proud, frightened) when you read that.
- I like the way you read it like the character was talking.
- You read it just like talking. Great!
- You paid careful attention to pacing (pausing, inflection/intonation, phrasing) to help you read with expression. Good work!

Expression: Characterization and Feelings

Objectives

Students will:

- use characters' words and actions to determine what they are like and how they feel
- demonstrate understanding of the text through purposeful expression
- use effective expression to make their reading sound like talking

---

Mini-Lesson BLM 14, page 49

Little Chick

Hen got up and counted her chicks. "Little Chick is gone!" she said. "Oh no, oh no!"

Hen ran to the barn. "Horse! Horse! Have you seen Little Chick?" she asked.

"No," said Horse. "Go ask Rabbit if he has seen her."

Hen ran to the field. "Rabbit! Rabbit! Have you seen Little Chick?"

"No," said Rabbit. "Has Frog seen her? Go ask him."

Hen ran to the pond. "Frog! Frog! Have you seen Little Chick?"

"Yes," said Frog. "She went to the pigpen with Little Pig."

Hen ran to the pigpen. Little Chick was playing with Little Pig. "Little Chick!" cried the hen.

Little Chick looked up. "Oh, were you looking for me?" she asked.

Anchor Chart

Expression

- We do not use the same tone of voice for everything we read.
- Our tone of voice should match the mood of the passage.
- We can figure out, or anticipate, the mood from the title and other clues.
- We use the author's or characters' words to confirm their feelings.
- Reading with expression helps the passage sound right and make sense.
- We use pacing, pausing, inflection/intonation, and phrasing to read with expression.

Introduce the Skill (10 minutes)

- **Say:** *We have learned that we use expression when we read. We use clues—such as the title, pictures, bold print, or punctuation—to figure out the mood of a passage. Some passages have quotation marks. When we see quotation marks, we need to think about what that story character is saying. The words, along with how the character acts, give us clues about what kind of person the character is and how he or she feels. We then try to make our voices sound the way that character might talk.*

- Display a transparency of the fluency mini-lesson passage BLM on the overhead and read the title. **Say:** *This is a story about a missing chick. The hen is very worried, so I will use a worried voice to read her parts. The farm animals try to help, so I will use a helpful voice for their parts. Little Chick is very surprised that everyone is looking for her, so I will use a surprised voice for her part. Reading the characters' words in these different ways will help the passage sound right and make sense.*

- Have students listen and follow along as you read the story aloud as described. Then **say:** *Now I will read the characters' parts showing different feelings. I will pretend everyone is angry.* Read the first three paragraphs as described. Then repeat with other feelings, such as pride, delight, or confusion.

- **Ask:** *Which way sounds the best? Why?*

- Reread the class Anchor Chart together to remind students how good readers read with expression. (See the example provided.)

Group Guided Practice (15 minutes)

- Distribute the BLM for *Little Chick*. Ask students to echo-read each sentence, and then have them choral-read the story with you. Next, allow the group to choral-read the story without your assistance.

- Distribute the Fluency Self-Assessment Master Checklist BLM from page 52. Then review the assessment criteria for expression and integration (see the checklist, right). Ask students to give a thumbs-up or thumbs-down on each question based on the group's choral-reading. Discuss their responses.

- Pair students and ask them to read *Little Chick* together one or more times.

- Ask students to rate themselves on specific fluency skills covered in this lesson using their master checklists.

- Check comprehension by asking students to summarize or retell the story to a partner.

MODEL SUMMARY

Little Chick was missing. Hen looked for Little Chick. The other farm animals tried to help. Hen finally found Little Chick playing with Little Pig. Little Chick was surprised that Hen was looking for her.

Individual/Partner Practice (15 minutes)

- Ask students to practice their oral reading skills by reading texts at their independent reading levels. You may want to use the leveled passages in Newmark Learning's Independent Fluency Practice Series.

- Carefully monitor students' progress, using the appropriate prompts (provided in the sidebar, right) to support their oral reading.

- Remind students to use the Self-Assessment Checklist to rate their oral reading skills and note any areas they might need to work on.

Performance (5 minutes)

- Invite individuals or partners to read a sentence or two from their fluency practice texts aloud for the class, paying special attention to reading with expression.

Self-Assessment Checklist

Expression

☐ Did I look for clues so I could anticipate the mood of the passage?

☐ Did I use my tone of voice, facial expressions, and body language to express what the author or characters were thinking or feeling?

☐ Did I change my reading when something new was about to happen?

Integration

☐ Did I read the words right?

☐ Did I read the words at the right speed?

☐ Did I read with expression?

☐ Did my reading sound like talking?

☐ Did I understand what I read?

Expression Prompts

Goal Oriented

- Let's read the title and look at the pictures. That will help us anticipate the mood of the passage.
- I see quotation marks, so the character is talking. I need to make my voice sound like the character's voice.
- I'll pretend to be that character. Listen to how I make my reading sound like he/she might talk.
- I need to make my voice, face, and body match what the author/character is saying when I read.
- Listen to me read this. Can you hear how excited (sad, proud, frightened) my voice sounds?

Directive and Corrective Feedback

- Make your voice sound excited (sad, proud, frightened).
- Make the character's voice match his/her actions and feelings.
- Read it like the author would say it.
- Repeat after me and read with expression.
- Use the punctuation to help you put expression in your voice.

Self-Monitoring and Reflection

- How did you know what tone of voice to use?
- Where did you read with expression?
- What part do you need to read again with more expression?
- Did you use pacing (pausing, inflection/ intonation, phrasing) to help you read with expression?

Validating and Confirming

- You noticed the funny pictures, so you used a happy tone of voice. Good!
- You sounded excited (sad, proud, frightened) when you read that.
- I like the way you read it like the character was talking.
- You read it just like talking. Great!
- You paid careful attention to pacing (pausing, inflection/intonation, phrasing) to help you read with expression. Good work!

Expression: Dramatic Expression

Objectives

Students will:

- utilize the skills of drama when they read

- demonstrate understanding of the text through purposeful expression

- use effective expression to make their reading sound like talking

---

Mini-Lesson BLM 15, page 50

One Misty, Moisty Morning

One misty, moisty morning,

when cloudy was the weather,

I chanced to meet an old man,

clothed all in leather.

He began to compliment

and I began to grin.

How do you do? And how do you do?

And how do you do again?

Anchor Chart

Expression

- We do not use the same tone of voice for everything we read.

- Our tone of voice should match the mood of the passage.

- We can figure out, or anticipate, the mood from the title and other clues.

- We use the author's or characters' words to confirm their feelings.

- Reading with expression helps the passage sound right and make sense.

- We use pacing, pausing, inflection/intonation, and phrasing to read with expression.

Introduce the Skill (10 minutes)

- **Say:** *We have learned that we use expression when we read. Features such as the title, pictures, bold print, and punctuation give us clues about the mood of a passage. The author's or characters' words and actions give us clues about what kind of people they are and how they think and feel. We then try to make our voices sound the way the author or character might talk in that situation. We use all the things we've learned about pacing, pausing, inflection/ intonation, and phrasing to help us read with expression. We can even use our faces and bodies to help us.*

- Display a transparency of the fluency mini-lesson passage BLM on the overhead and read the title. **Say:** *This is a poem. I will read the poem with dramatic expression. That means I will use all the clues in the poem to help my voice, face, and body show and tell the meaning of the poem. Reading the poem with dramatic expression will help the poem sound right and make sense.*

- Have students listen and follow along as you read the story aloud as described. Then **say:** *Now I will read the poem without paying attention to the clues and without using my voice, face, and body to help me. Listen closely.* Read the poem all the way through in a dull monotone.

- **Ask:** *Which way sounds the best? Which way is easiest to understand? Why?*

- Reread the class Anchor Chart together to remind students how good readers read with expression. (See the example provided.)

Group Guided Practice (15 minutes)

- Distribute the BLM for *One Misty, Moisty Morning.* Ask students to echo-read each line, and then have them choral-read the poem with you. Next, allow the group to choral-read the poem without your assistance.

- Distribute the Fluency Self-Assessment Master Checklist BLM from page 52. Then review the assessment criteria for expression and integration (see the checklist, right). Ask students to give a thumbs-up or thumbs-down on each question based on the group's choral-reading. Discuss their responses.

- Pair students and ask them to read *One Misty, Moisty Morning* together one or more times.

- Ask students to rate themselves on specific fluency skills covered in this lesson using their master checklists.

- Check comprehension by asking student partners to discuss the following: *What three words describe the weather in this poem?* (misty, moisty, cloudy) *Were the two people in the poem polite to each other? How do you know?* (Yes. They said "How do you do?" to each other.)

Individual/Partner Practice (15 minutes)

- Ask students to practice their oral reading skills by reading texts at their independent reading levels. You may want to use the leveled passages in Newmark Learning's Independent Fluency Practice Series.

- Carefully monitor students' progress, using the appropriate prompts (provided in the sidebar, right) to support their oral reading.

- Remind students to use the Self-Assessment Checklist to rate their oral reading skills and note any areas they might need to work on.

Performance (5 minutes)

- Invite individuals or partners to read a sentence or two from their fluency practice texts aloud for the class, paying special attention to reading with expression.

Self-Assessment Checklist

Expression

- ☐ Did I look for clues so I could anticipate the mood of the passage?
- ☐ Did I use my tone of voice, facial expressions, and body language to express what the author or characters were thinking or feeling?
- ☐ Did I change my reading when something new was about to happen?

Integration

- ☐ Did I read the words right?
- ☐ Did I read the words at the right speed?
- ☐ Did I read with expression?
- ☐ Did my reading sound like talking?
- ☐ Did I understand what I read?

Expression Prompts

Goal Oriented

- Let's read the title and look at the pictures. That will help us anticipate the mood of the passage.
- I see quotation marks, so the character is talking. I need to make my voice sound like the character's voice.
- I'll pretend to be that character. Listen to how I make my reading sound like he/she might talk.
- I need to make my voice, face, and body match what the author/character is saying when I read.
- Listen to me read this. Can you hear how excited (sad, proud, frightened) my voice sounds?

Directive and Corrective Feedback

- Make your voice sound excited (sad, proud, frightened).
- Make the character's voice match his/her actions and feelings.
- Read it like the author would say it.
- Repeat after me and read with expression.
- Use the punctuation to help you put expression in your voice.

Self-Monitoring and Reflection

- How did you know what tone of voice to use?
- Where did you read with expression?
- What part do you need to read again with more expression?
- Did you use pacing (pausing, inflection/intonation, phrasing) to help you read with expression?

Validating and Confirming

- You noticed the funny pictures, so you used a happy tone of voice. Good!
- You sounded excited (sad, proud, frightened) when you read that.
- I like the way you read it like the character was talking.
- You read it just like talking Great!
- You paid careful attention to pacing (pausing, inflection/intonation, phrasing) to help you read with expression. Good work!

Miss Mary Mack

Miss Mary Mack, Mack, Mack
All dressed in black, black, black
With silver buttons, buttons, buttons
All down her back, back, back.

She asked her mother, mother, mother
For fifty cents, cents, cents
To see the elephant, elephant, elephant
Jump the fence, fence, fence.

He jumped so high, high, high
He touched the sky, sky, sky
And didn't come back, back, back
Till the fourth of July, July, July.

Paper Cup Telephone

1. Get two paper cups. Get a pushpin. Get some string.

2. Poke a hole in the bottom of each paper cup.

3. Wiggle the pushpin to make the holes a little bigger.

4. Put the string through the holes.

5. Tie knots in the ends of the string.

6. Hand one cup to a partner. Tell your partner to listen in the cup.

7. Stretch out the string. Talk into your cup.

8. Now let your partner talk to you. You've made a paper cup telephone!

Things I Like To Do

Speaker 1: I like to go for long walks with my dog.

Speaker 2: I like to run in the yard with my dog.

Speaker 1: I like to play board games that take all afternoon.

Speaker 2: I like to play computer games with lots of action. Wham! Zam!

Speaker 1: I like to bake cookies with my granddad.

Speaker 2: I like to grab a quick burger with my big brother.

Speaker 1: I like to learn new words. Today I learned to say au-to-bi-o-gra-phy.

Speaker 2: I like words, too. Did you know that some people say soda and some people say pop?

Speaker 1 and **Speaker 2:** Y . . . a . . . w . . . n. I like to take a nap. See you later!

Snow

Many people like snow.

Kids like to go sledding, build a snowman, and throw snowballs.

People take lots of pictures because the trees look so pretty.

People can ski on the fresh snow, called powder.

Snowplow drivers have to work hard, but they feel good helping people.

Some people don't like snow, though.

Snow makes things harder for mail carriers, farmers, builders, and pilots.

Do you like snow?

Knock-Knock Jokes

Reader 1: Knock, knock.

Reader 2: Who's there?

Reader 1: Ben.

Reader 2: Ben who?

Reader 1: Ben knocking on the door all afternoon!

Reader 1: Knock, knock.

Reader 2: Who's there?

Reader 1: Isadore.

Reader 2: Isadore who?

Reader 1: Isadore made out of wood?

Reader 1: Knock, knock.

Reader 2: Who's there?

Reader 1: Norma Lee.

Reader 2: Norma Lee who?

Reader 1: Norma Lee I'd use the doorbell, but it's broken!

Little Boy Blue

Little Boy Blue

Come blow your horn.

The sheep's in the meadow

The cow's in the corn.

And where is the boy who looks after the sheep?

He's under the haystack, fast asleep.

Student Interview

Teacher: What's your favorite animal?

Student: I like my dog. He's a Chocolate Lab named Brownie.

Teacher: What's your favorite pair of shoes?

Student: I like my brown shoes. They're the color of chocolate.

Teacher: What's your favorite part of school?

Student: I like lunchtime. Sometimes my mom packs a chocolate bar in my lunch box.

Teacher: I think I know the answer to the next question. What's your favorite flavor of ice cream?

Student: I like vanilla. Surprise!

The Hungry Fox

Fox went to the farm. He wanted to eat Rooster.

Cow got up. "Shoo, Fox, shoo!" said Cow. "Go away! Come back some other day."

Sheep got up. "Shoo, Fox, shoo!" said Sheep. "Go away! Come back some other day."

Pig got up. "Shoo, Fox, shoo!" said Pig. "Go away! Come back some other day."

Rooster got up. "Cock-a-doodle-doo!" said Rooster.

The farmer got up. "Shoo, Fox, shoo!" said the farmer. "Go away, and do NOT come back some other day!"

Tiny Tim

I had a little puppy.
His name was Tiny Tim.
I put him in the bathtub
To see if he could swim.

He drank up all the water.
He ate a bar of soap.
The next thing I knew,
He had a bubble in his throat.

In came the doctor,
In came the nurse,
In came the lady with the alligator purse.

"Mumps!" said the doctor.
"Measles!" said the nurse.
"Hiccups!" said the lady with the
alligator purse.

Out went the doctor.
Out went the nurse.
Out went the lady with the alligator purse.

Bus Trip

Group 1: Look for some people.

Group 2: How many people?

Group 1: A number of people.

Group 2: What will they do?

Group 1: Get on the bus.

Group 2: Could you go? You and I?

Group 1: We will go. Now is the time.

Group 2: We will go. From here to there.

Group 1 and **Group 2:** This is a good day!

Silly Zoo

The bear had no hair.
The cubs sat in tubs.
The cow took a bow.
The goat wore a coat.

The deer gave a cheer.
The seal wasn't real.
The fish made a wish.
The bat wore a hat.

The snake liked to bake.
The birds said long words.
The lion was cryin',
But the giraffe . . . had to laugh!

How Many Puddles?

Juan counted puddles on the way to school.

"I see a puddle in my yard," said Juan. Juan walked through the first puddle.

"I see a puddle at the corner," said Juan. Juan skipped through the second puddle.

"I see a puddle by the fence," said Juan. Juan hopped through the third puddle.

"I see a puddle under the flagpole," said Juan. Juan ran through the fourth puddle.

Juan went into his classroom. "I saw four puddles on the way to school," he said.

"I see a puddle IN the school," said the teacher.

Juan looked down. Water dripped from his shoes.

"Oops!" said Juan. "That makes five puddles!"

Treasure Island?

An island is land with water all the way around it. Ships go by the island.

Sometimes things fall off the ships. The things float to the island. People find the things on the beach!

One island in the North Sea is call Terschelling (ter-SKEL-ing). People may soon call it Treasure Island, though. Strange things are always floating to this island!

One time, people found lots of sweaters on the beach. Another time, they found lots of tennis shoes. Another time they found lots of children's toys.

Yesterday, a ship was in a storm. Lots of bananas fell off the ship. People found the bananas on the beach.

The people talked about the bananas. "They might be a little salty!" some people said.

What will the people do with all those bananas? "We could send them to a zoo!" said one man on the beach.

Little Chick

Hen got up and counted her chicks. "Little Chick is gone!" she said. "Oh no, oh no!"

Hen ran to the barn. "Horse! Horse! Have you seen Little Chick?" she asked.

"No," said Horse. "Go ask Rabbit if he has seen her."

Hen ran to the field. "Rabbit! Rabbit! Have you seen Little Chick?"

"No," said Rabbit. "Has Frog seen her? Go ask him."

Hen ran to the pond. "Frog! Frog! Have you seen Little Chick?"

"Yes," said Frog. "She went to the pigpen with Little Pig."

Hen ran to the pigpen. Little Chick was playing with Little Pig. "Little Chick!" cried the hen.

Little Chick looked up. "Oh, were you looking for me?" she asked.

One Misty, Moisty Morning

One misty, moisty morning,

when cloudy was the weather,

I chanced to meet an old man,

clothed all in leather.

He began to compliment

and I began to grin.

How do you do? And how do you do?

And how do you do again?

Student Name: _____ Date: _____

The key elements of reading fluency—accuracy, speed, pacing, pausing, inflection/intonation, expression, phrasing, and the integration of these skills—may be assessed any time a student reads aloud. Discuss the assessment rubric, modeling each description, so students know what you expect.

Fluency Rubric

Rating Scale	Elements of Fluent Reading
	Accuracy
1	Multiple attempts at decoding words are unsuccessful. Word reading accuracy is inadequate/poor, below 90%.
2	Attempts to self-correct errors are usually unsuccessful. Word reading accuracy is marginal, between 90–93%.
3	Attempts to self-correct errors are successful. Word reading accuracy is good, between 94–97%.
4	Most words are read correctly on initial attempt. Minimal self-corrections, all successful. Word reading accuracy is excellent, 98–100%.
	Rate: Speed, Pacing, Pausing
1	Reading is slow and laborious.
2	Reading is either moderately slow or inappropriately fast, and pausing is infrequent or ignored.
3	Reading is an unbalanced combination of slow and fast reading containing inconsistent pausing.
4	Reading is consistently natural, conversational, and appropriately varied (resembling natural oral language).
	Prosody: Inflection/Intonation and Expression
1	Reads in an inexpressive, monotone manner and does not attend to punctuation.
2	Reads with some intonation (pitch/tone/volume/stress) and some attention to punctuation. Reads in a monotone at times.
3	Reads by adjusting intonation (pitch/tone/volume/stress) inappropriately. Consistently attends to punctuation.
4	Reads with intonation that reflects feeling, anticipation, tension, character development, and mood.
	Prosody: Phrasing
1	Reads word by word. Does not attend to author's syntax or sentence structures. Has limited sense of phrase boundaries.
2	Reads slowly and in a choppy manner, usually in two-word phrases. Some attention is given to author's syntax and sentence structures.
3	Reads in phrases of three to four words. Appropriate syntax is used.
4	Reads in longer, more meaningful phrases. Regularly uses phrase boundaries, punctuation, sentence structure, and author's syntax to reflect comprehension and fluent reading.
	Integration
1	Reading is monotone, laborious, inexpressive, and accuracy rate is poor, below 90%.
2	Reading is unbalanced with inconsistent rate and pacing, some phrasing, inadequate intonation and expression, marginal accuracy, between 90–93%.
3	Reading is somewhat adjusted with some variation in rate, appropriate prosody, and with good accuracy, between 94–97%.
4	Reads in an integrated manner with high accuracy, rate, intonation, and expression on a consistent basis. Fluent reading reflects understanding and interpretation of text.

Fluency Self-Assessment Master Checklist

☺ ☹

Speed/Pacing

Did my speed and pacing match the kind of text I was reading? ☐ ☐

Did my speed and pacing match what the author was saying? ☐ ☐

Did I read with a natural talking voice? ☐ ☐

Did I slow my reading down when appropriate? ☐ ☐

Did I pay attention to punctuation? ☐ ☐

Pausing

Did I pause to keep from running all my words together? ☐ ☐

Did I pause in the correct locations? ☐ ☐

Did I pause for the appropriate length of time? ☐ ☐

Did I pause to help my reading make sense? ☐ ☐

Did I use punctuation to help me figure out when to pause? ☐ ☐

Inflection/Intonation

Did I make my voice rise at a question mark? ☐ ☐

Did I make my voice fall at a period? ☐ ☐

Did I think about what the author was saying so I would
know when to read louder or softer? ☐ ☐

Did I think about what the author was saying so I would know
when to stress or emphasize words? ☐ ☐

Phrasing

Did I notice the phrases? ☐ ☐

Did I read all the words in each phrase together? ☐ ☐

Did I think about what the words in the phrase mean when
they are together? ☐ ☐

Expression

Did I look for clues so I could anticipate the mood of the passage? ☐ ☐

Did I use my tone of voice, facial expressions, and body language
to express what the author or characters were thinking or feeling? ☐ ☐

Did I change my reading when something new was about to happen? ☐ ☐

Integration

Did I read the words right? (accuracy) ☐ ☐

Did I read the words at the right speed? (rate) ☐ ☐

Did I read with expression? (prosody) ☐ ☐

Did my reading sound like talking? ☐ ☐

Did I understand what I read? ☐ ☐